AF597255

BOTTOMLESS SURFACE

"Not all depths are hidden; some are found in the space between breaths"

Sameer Chettri

INDIA • SINGAPORE • MALAYSIA

ISBN
Paperback 979-8-89632-770-7
Hardcase 979-8-89724-264-1

CONTENTS

BOTTOMLESS SURFACE

This book is a heartfelt journey through 16 years of my life, starting all the way back in 2008—an era when keypad phones ruled the world, and typing a text felt like cracking some secret code. Each poem is a window into moments both profound and bizarre, capturing life's twists and turns in ways I hope will surprise and resonate with you.

I humbly invite you, dear reader, to dive into this collection and enjoy the flow of thoughts I've carefully crafted—sometimes poetic, sometimes just me in conversation with myself.

Feel free to interpret my perspective in your own way, there's no right or wrong here! And if you feel inspired (or even slightly annoyed), I'm all ears for your feedback. Criticism is welcome too—after all, a little sarcasm is healthier than modern diets. Just remember, constructive criticism builds bridges; blunt criticism… well, it builds thicker skin! So, go ahead, flip the pages, and let's see where this adventure takes us!

Thank you in advance for dedicating your time to exploring this book. Your time and attention are sincerely appreciated!

Travel safe,

Sameer

PREFACE

"Take pride in not knowing everything, for it leaves some room to learn more! Possess something formless which is beyond getting stolen from you. And once you possess it, do remember to share it with the ones who already know. The only way to truly keep it forever with you is to just let it go"

~Sameer Chettri

1

ACCEPTANCE – PRESENT TENSE

During times of change, it's always the resistance
that gives rise to conflict over time.
It's not about stepping over old ideas and beliefs,
but about stepping up to new ones with new possibilities.

In the shifting sands of what we know,
we must embrace the ebb, let it flow.
With each new dawn comes the chance to grow,
to weave fresh dreams into the fabric we sew.

Let go of the weight that anchors the heart,
for in acceptance, we find a new start.
The winds of change may howl and roar,
but they also open wide a welcoming door.

So, breathe in the moment, let the past fade,
in the dance of now, let fears be unmade.
For life's vibrant palette invites us to see
the beauty in change, the strength in being free.

2

INNOCENT IGNORANCE

Innocent ignorance, so pure and mild,
Behind your smile, there's someone beguiled.
I was thrilled to see you, but now I'm unsure,
Was it really you? I can't be sure.

I turned from reality, yet felt you near,
The scene is clear now, but tinged with fear—
A little dark, but distant still,
Living in the past, against my will.

A ghost that haunts, though not alive,
I tremble, wishing I could revive.
As if in terror, I avoid the view,
I only wish I could remember you.

3

AT THE EDGE OF THOUGHT

It slips beyond what feels real,
a dream that drifts, impossible to steal.
A smile melts into a flowing stream,
where hope and life blend like a dream.

The wind carries us to unknown skies,
life seen through ever-changing eyes.
Love is a gift, rare and profound,
like the sky meeting the solid ground.

The sun sets only to rise again,
and truth lies clear in the gaze of a friend.
Some words turn to music we hear,
if we believe in magic, simple and clear.

Our hearts beat steady, loyal, and strong,
yet fragile enough to break before long.
We live, we love, then drift away—
to where? No one can say.

4

PRESENCE OF YOUR ABSENCE

What is the point of a candle's flame,
When night has gone, and dawn is tame?
The light of the heavens leaves me in pain,
lost in shadows I can't explain.

Is it dawn's glow or a question unclear?
Waves make circles as the sky draws near.
The horizon feels so far and wide,
and every step is hard to stride.

The stars all shine in the depth of your eyes,
your quiet words drown the noise of the skies.
Memories return, bringing back old times,
as the sun blurs the line between real and divine.

5

ALONE IN THE SEA OF FACES

Best memories locked away,
Hidden from the light of day,
To create fear, just a guise,
To control the strength that lies.

We've taken much from one another,
And in the process, lost each other.
Born with power to shape our fate,
Yet we always seek to imitate.

If life's purpose is just to live,
why does death seem like the gift?
If eyes were made to embrace the light,
then why do we question their sight?

6

THE ART OF DISCUSSION

From an argument to conflict, from quarrel to fight,
from chaos to riot, to battle, and finally to war,
a healthy discussion remains the art
that is taken for granted from the very start.

Words can build bridges or walls that divide,
but in open dialogue, true understanding can thrive.
Listening with intention, speaking with care,
creates a space where all voices can share.

When we approach with kindness, seeking to learn,
the flames of discord can soften and burn.
Ideas take flight when nurtured with grace,
transforming conflict into a productive space.

So let us cherish this art, not let it fade,
for in every conversation, a new path is laid.
Through patience and respect, let's find common ground,
in the rhythm of dialogue, harmony is found.

7

DREAMS WITHIN REACH – A TRIBUTE TO MY MOTHER

As I lay my empty head beside her,

My blurry dream becomes so clear.

And I find no reason to be in fear;

My bodily afflictions don't last when I see her.

As I place my fractured heart beside her,

My farthest dream seems so near.

And my bodily afflictions flow out with tears,

I wish I could always wake up to see her.

8

793001

Beneath the pines, the plateaus sleep,
where clouds gather and secrets keep.
The sun retreats, the waterfalls sing,
and fresh dew scents the air like spring.

A place of calm, where birds take flight,
gliding softly in the golden light.
Mist caresses my windowpane,
as rain performs its quiet gain.

Even lost, we find a guiding star,
hope renews, no matter where we are.
With smiles for strangers and kindness shown,
we honor each soul, and feel at home.

Home is where hearts find their tune,
voices blending beneath the moon.
Here, in the hills where peace has grown,
I've found my heart, my home, my own.

9

REVERSE HORIZONS

Frozen sea or stagnant cloud,
The silence speaks, too loud.
Vision clear, but doubt fills my mind,
Still searching, unsure of what I'll find.

Hopes aren't as vast as the sky,
Moving backward, yet I try.
Each day unfolds, but words are blurred,
I look back, but truths unheard.

Paths once walked, shadows of the past,
Caught in time, it slips too fast.
The horizon shifts, promises fade,
Tethered to thoughts that never trade.

In stillness, I seek life's pulse,
A reminder of struggles, of birth's impulse.
Can I trust this journey, even when I am lost?
Is movement worth it, no matter the cost?

Perhaps the key lies in what I've learned,

In the flicker of hope that still burns.

With each step, strength is found,

Even in reverse, beauty surrounds.

10

CONTRAILS IN MY SKY

You fly so high, tethered to my heart,
Innumerable reasons for us to be apart.
You may disappear high above the cloud,
And then reappear in the sky, without a doubt.

As you leave the ground to gain altitude,
I get busy down here, grounded in solitude.
I know the turbulence frightens you the most;
It's just the air pockets, not a ghost.

I find myself cruising in thoughts without a clue,
Talking to myself for hours about you.
As I approach landing in reality,
I will still be thinking of you in surreality.

I spread my wings to catch you in the air,
To be by your side, just anytime, anywhere.
But I have now found myself to be yours;
There is nothing less and nothing more.

1 1

BREAKING OF NOISE INTO THE SILENCE

Molten rocks roll across an icy plane,
joy evolving, leaving no pain.
Day hides beneath the night's dark shroud,
a smile masks a frown to appease the crowd.
Thunder rumbles when rain takes its leave,
echoes of doubt in the mind we weave.

Fear of floods pushed us to the skies,
but tears drowned us all, with open eyes.
The glitter of glamour steals nature's glow,
marring the grace we've ceased to know.
Purer than truth in the eyes of a liar,
every hope and dream burn in the funeral pyre.

Stay in your shoes, to be yourself,
while trying to be you, I almost lost myself.
Hold your bemused smile like cracks on a wall,
stretching endlessly yet standing tall.

Search for answers, near or far,
you'll find them waiting where you are.

Never shy from what makes you grow;
you're a statue of art, more than you know.

1 2

BLESSED ENOUGH

Your presence in my life is enough; you are a blessing.
Yet, still, I can't get enough of you for myself,
Knowing that you belong to yourself, too.
How can I envy you for having more of you to keep,
Only to pour it over me?

What if my heart demands too much?
What if my love becomes a shadow,
Darkening the light I cherish in you?
Still, your essence flows through me,
A river of warmth that nourishes my soul.

So, I breathe in the moments we share,
Each glance, each smile, a treasure to keep.
I am blessed to witness your journey,
Even as I wish to walk beside you,
To intertwine our paths in a dance of souls.

Your presence in my life is enough; you are a blessing,

And as I release my grasp, I find the peace,

That in loving you fully, I become more of myself,

Embracing the beautiful tension,

In this sacred space where we both belong.

1 3

VEILS OF SHADOWS

I cannot grasp what I've always feared,
a ghost that never truly appeared.
It slips into mist, a shadow unseen,
a dark white shadow, haunting in between.

The moon dissolves in a cloud's cold hold,
while bare trees whisper secrets untold.
Night's creatures stir, prowling the deep,
as my shallow heart falters in its beat.

Yet breath persists, defying sense,
neither alive nor free of existence.
I've pierced each fragile, unreal desire,
trapped within a mind reshaped by dire.

14

IN FRONT OF THE BACK

Crumpled, cast aside like a paper ball,
too flawed, too plain for a perfect world.
The weight of hate I cannot bear,
love buried deep where none can stare.

Morning's light fades thin and frail,
as my shattered boat drifts without sail.
Secrets linger beneath the tide,
a broken smile hides the ache inside.

A heart of stone, brittle and weak,
I whisper to shadows when I seek.
Peace takes flight, leaving hope undone,
reality, a dream, unraveled, spun.

15

WHISPERS OF THE UNCONSCIOUS

I drift into sleep, dreams unfolding unseen,
their meaning is a mystery, soft and serene.
In a vast world of oceans and endless land,
I wander alone, searching for a hand.

Morning's breath, so gentle, so pure,
whispers a hymn I can't ignore.
For just a moment, I leave it behind,
a love as eternal as a mother's bind.

But as I lean back, winter takes hold,
freezing my spirit, icy and cold.
My hollow heart beats, echoing pain,
as boiling thoughts pour like torrential rain.

Joy flies like birds, vanishing fast,
leaving me breathing the air so vast,
poisoned and thick, yet mountains stand tall,
I scream in silence, hoping to hear your call.

My hands, they tremble, digging the dirt,

as fear of death ignites life's worth.

They warned me, "Don't look up, or you'll fall,"

but I dared to gaze—and found answers in it all.

1 6

ECHOES OF EXISTENCE

I am a word, beautiful but empty inside,
a shell of stone where my feelings hide.
Ageless and unseen, I wander alone,
even the mirror won't show what's my own.

I am a fire that never feels heat,
a scream in the dark no one will meet.
Frozen water that cannot flow,
I rise higher the deeper I go.

I am hunger with no desire to feed,
a journey through life with no end to meet.
A sickness born in the purest air,
a quiet poison lingering there.

I am a mask with a hairline crack,
a fragile world where illusions stack.
A soul in rest, yet still on life's stage,
playing endless roles through every age.

17
THE SILENT COLLAPSE

The fireflies' glow has faded away,
and life keeps moving, day by day.
The river, once deep and full of blue,
is now cracked, lifeless, with no hue.

I used to have dreams I wanted to share,
but now I'm stuck in a nightmare's snare.
Silence surrounds me, I can't understand,
life feels empty when greed's in command.

Tears once moved hearts, made them care,
but now no leaves stir when I despair.
I once walked freely, bold and bright,
but now I'm weighed down by fear and fright.

Trees that sheltered birds and squirrels,
have been replaced by steel and pearls.
The horizon once endless, full of grace,
now fades away in a crowded space.

18

RULED BY TIME

Infant birds staring at the sky,

Unaware that they must eventually fly.

Blue heaven with no boundaries or walls,

And no nest to catch them when they fall.

The bottomless pit within the heart

Keeps the weary mind always apart.

Gusts of wind never lets the clouds settle;

A new day is an enemy, and life is a battle.

This one is dedicated to my beloved friend – Dr. Ivan Challam – Mr. Hyde as we called him

19

NOCTURNAL EMBRACE

Darkness brightens my way,
I see the sky filled with diamonds.
Like snow covering the hay,
You sleep at night; I sleep during the day.

One single revolution makes it your day,
What you see are fictions and illusions.
No matter if it's March, April, or May,
My day is night, and my night is day.

They say the night is claimed by the dark,
But angels shine with a guiding spark.
On doomsday, to whom will you turn?
For in the silence, your soul will yearn.

20

THE ILLUSION OF TRUTH

What I remember are fleeting memories,
Fragments that fade, too few to hold tight.
I wish silence would fill my ears,
But all I hear are tales, far from right.

Each day teaches a new, disguised lesson,
Yet we pretend we've learned nothing at all.
No wall can touch the endless sky,
Still, we fight for nations, feeling small.

What I see are fleeting illusions,
My words scrawled in desperate haste.
I seek connection, yet remain apart,
Living a life of solitude, misplaced.

Every truth feels like a hidden lie,
And we're all just here to buy and sell.
Praise may come once we're gone from sight,
But in the end, all is the story we tell.

21

THE ESSENCE UNSPOKEN

The sky stretches wide, endless and free,

A constant presence, as clouds drift gently.

I watch them move, but the space stays the same,

A timeless beauty, like an eternal flame.

From where I stand, I look up in awe,

At the heavens above, and the peace they draw.

The sky is the roof of the world we know,

Embracing the earth with a gentle glow.

As I think about the life I hold,

I realize its value is worth more than gold—

More than sand slipping through my hand,

For true worth can't be measured by land.

22

THE MODERN WORLD

Sacrificial nights of restless sleep,
Frozen tears from those bleeding eyes.
The piercing pain of broken ribs,
Warriors of the battle face demise.

Crime enslaves the world so wide,
Peace shattered, torn inside.
Countless hopes that fall apart,
A sickness cast from every heart.

Every mind grows out of fear,
A deadly threat to its own kind.
Laws of the culprits victimize the innocent;
Saints in front, serpents behind.

Diversion from factual reality,
Masterminds brought to slavery.
Crisis—everything here is sold.
The planet bearing life is now the modern world.

23

UNDEFINED

For the flames of agony to rise within, the cause is undefined,
For the darkest clouds to linger, haunting the mind,
And your dead heart, with treasures of hope untamed,
Remains unclaimed, still waiting, unnamed.

The distant sun dries the sea of life, to create anew,
Fear lives where faith is absent, known to but a few.
Joy and sorrow lie beside you—what will you choose?
For life's certainty, so uncertain, the reason's still obscure,

Finding peace only beyond this life, the cause is undefined.
Bliss in ignorance, its reason undefined,
All of this, a mystery, concealed in the mind.

***Poem title - suggested by my friend Aaron Landor Chyne Massar – twisted_deranged_angel*

24

REFLECTIONS AT DUSK

Why feel low when the sun is going down,
When we know it will soon be around?
The cure is loneliness,
And we all live in the middle of some town.

You smile like a fracture in stillness,
Lips parting—clouds unfurling in silence.
Rays slip through the sky, yet shadows rise,
Doubts stretch endlessly, unseen, unwise.

Once life drifted, now it sways with weight,
Trust lingers in cracks, elusive, late.
Steps fade, bold yet distant, cold,
Truth murmurs, untold, in the void it unfolds.

25

THE GRAVE OF ASPIRATIONS

Heaven feels distant, no longer near,
Words we speak are clouded with fear.
Hands once reached for peace and light,
Now grasp for power in endless fight.

The cries of nature are hushed by our greed,
We, the stewards of a world in need.
Leaves fall gently, branches bow,
Wounds on the earth, we've caused somehow.

Truth is hidden and lies take their place.
A generation sleeps, lost in space.
Anger and sorrow fuel the flames,
The birth of hope, yet nothing remains.

The soul is pulled towards endless strife,
A restless mind, seeking a quiet life.
A ship of dreams drifts through the fire,
A world undone by unquenched desire.

26

APRIL FLOWER: PCD

Dying makes no sense, as it leads to complete numbness
and the absence of pain to feel alive.
Inevitably, I come close to death,
only when I think of you not being in my life.
Breathing shallow with a heavy load on my chest,
waiting for the sun rays to strike my face with your smile.

The human spirit is filled with passion,
and my only passion is to be under the spell of your charm forever.
I don't know what love truly is,
as we have all been confused by it at least once in our lifetime.
All I know and truly believe is,
what's shared between you and me is divine.

27

BOUNDLESS AFFECTION

Your care spreads like ocean waves,
Deeper than the heart's vast graves.
Your words, a branch of endless tree;
In your heart, I am set free.

When the stars are out of my sight,
And the sky is no longer bright,
Of all those feelings, I hide—
I just want to be by your side.

I will find you even if I go blind.
I may get lost in the winds of time,
But you will still be on my mind.
I wish I could be a particle of dust;
In your light, all else turns to rust.

Rays of the sun make me blink;
This ship of hope will never sink.
Into those eyes, I always dive—
The only thing I do to survive.

28
THE JOURNEY TOWARDS LIGHT

Nothing stays the same, but change brings growth,
Beyond my gaze lies a world unknown,
The hands of time create new ways,
As joy flows on, lighting brighter days.

No road leads to perfect certainty,
But living fully is life's true decree,
Through every twist, we rise and strive,
In each moment, we feel alive.

Though we may not see beyond this life,
The journey itself is free from strife.
We shed old ways to grow anew,
And in each heart, hope shines through.

Life is a gift, a story to unfold,
A chance to learn, to love, to be bold.
The world is ours to shape and guide,
With kindness, let's walk side by side.

Truth and hope are the flames we carry,
With open eyes, the future is not scary.

29

LESSONS OF SOLITUDE

From the lowest mountain peak,
Across the clouds, I seek
The peaceful truth to be,
The person that hides inside of me.

Missing both friends and foe,
Living away from those I know,
Strange faces look familiar;
Grief and joy seem so similar.

How long shall the wheel roll?
An endless road my destiny holds.
Climbing the ladder to new heights,
Sleep is gone, and everything is white.

As I think, my feelings boil;
In very few minds, I dwell.
Thoughts unravel, deep and wild,
In quiet corners, I remain exiled.

3 0

SPECTERS OF THE SOUL

Every breath I take, I fade away,
Feeling joy has become hard to stay.
A stone that dreams of taking flight,
I'm blind, yet my thoughts burn bright.

To lose is to find hope anew,
I won your heart, but it's hollow too.
My hands are bound, tied with invisible ropes,
Holding my soul in a prison of hopes.

Round and round, the cycle goes,
Where I hide, only darkness knows.
From where I come, the cold winds blow,
A place where forgotten dreams may grow.

To believe, I need a reason why,
Yet every reason shifts and passes by.
There's no wrong in just being me,
I feel the ghost that's setting me free.

Bright light casts shadows in the night,
Enlightening the sorrow that feels so right.
The way we parted was cruel and sharp,
I built your grave inside my heart.

31

BEYOND REDEMPTION

No destiny can be described on a map,
Cradle of a child on his mother's lap.
We describe our feelings with that word,
But the cry of a bird is never heard.

Lost with the sunset and rising with the moon,
Born with no hands but a silver spoon.
A tree with huge branches and no roots,
I fell from a great height just for a while,

Dived from the mountain and ran into the woods.
Lost my balance when I saw you smile.
A hand is worthless without its fingers;
Knowledge grows, and wisdom lingers.

When life is lost, only sorrow weeps,
And words spoken leave blood upon the lips.
Death is real only with time;
Killing for judgment is still a crime.

3 2

VOICES OF THE VOID

Mist from the rain creates the rainbow,
Mind captivated by words so hollow.
I wish I could float in space,
Far, far away from the human race.

My bed is the earth, and stone is my pillow,
And I hear voices from below.
The dawn of darkness is by my side,
Dreaming of reality with eyes open wide.

The sky is painted with stars and secrets untold,
The land scarred by wars of old.
Ambush awaits in the days ahead,
Lay down your weapons, let nature be led.

3 3

CIRCLES OF THOUGHTS

Begin where the day ends,
A cycle spun in endless bends.
A weight unseen drapes my soul,
Pulled tight, yet I cannot control.
The mind, a blur between night and light,
Half asleep, half caught in flight.

I reach for the sky, yet touch the air,
Clouds weave distractions, but I'm aware.
And lightning burns my fingertips,
To end that relationship.

When I turn back, it's front again—
Meaningless words strike my head.
When I get pleasure, I feel the pain.
I walk the desert, but my feet are wet.

Is it the start or is it the end?
I might be trapped in thoughts that bend.
I'll bite my tongue rather to pretend,
We try to preserve, but all things descend.

34

BEAUTY BEYOND UNDERSTANDING

In ugliness, there lies a charm,

A beauty hidden in the storm.

Pride wears a crown, yet it falls on the ground,

A whisper lost, in a world so round.

Thoughts stretch beyond the endless skies,

Too late to see the truth behind the lies.

Words fill the mind, yet hands are still,

Voices rise where silence spills.

The pull of darkness, unseen, untold,

A beauty untouched, yet pure and bold.

3 5

LIGHT AND SHADOWS

Mist from the rain paints the rainbow,
While empty words in the mind echo.
I wish to drift in the vast, silent space,
Far from the world, away from the human race.

The sky whispers in colors we can't hear,
Shadows and light drawing near.
I long to escape, to be free and clear,
In the quiet of space, with nothing to fear.

36

THE SILENCE OF AWARENESS

The ability to realize my own unawareness,
Sheltering behind the veil of ignorance.
Bending the reality inside my head,
By the rays of light entering my eyes.

Seething with worry, then bursting,
The weightlessness of air quenching my thirst.
Where do I stop? Before I can even begin,
To let my thoughts flow in reverse.

If you can hear me, just turn down the volume;
Yet I can see you dreaming of peace.
Stay blind to remain unworried
About what's coming to comfort you.

37

INWARD JOURNEY

What others make you feel is not true,
And what you feel about them is just you.
Not a single drop of rain escapes gravity once fallen,
Nor do you always get back what's been stolen from you.

What you feel about yourself may not be you;
It's when your sleep takes away your dream,
To find someone new within you.
The whispers of doubt echo in your mind,
Yet the strength to rise is what you must find.

Peel back the layers, let the truth unfold,
For within your heart lies a spirit bold.
Embrace the silence, let the chaos cease,
In the journey inward, you'll find your peace.

With every breath, let go of the past,
Release the burdens that hold you fast.
In the depths of your soul, let love ignite,
And turn your inner darkness into light.

Explore the depths, let your spirit soar,

For the journey within is what you're searching for.

What others make you feel is not true,

Embrace your essence, and let it brew.

38

UNFELT YET SEEN

Shifting shades of glimmering shine,
Of the moon over the sands of time.
Melting clouds into the rain,
By the rays of the sun unchained.

Wind sweeps the dust into our eyes,
Leaving us in twinge to make us wise.
Imagine it's all happening in your dream;
You will then find yourself in a state of being.

A state of being awake wherein
You are detached from the reality that's fake.
When joy flies away like a bird, leaving no hope,
Breath becomes lifeless, like inhaling smoke.

The smoke of burning desires for you to choke upon;
It's never too late until you turn against yourself.
Time is a gift that will cost you your life—

So fragile is the life we trust,

I wish we had the roots to adjust,

But life, confined within this frame,

Is all we know, it's all the same.

39

PATHS OF PERCEPTION

The way we know ourselves always differs
From the way they perceive us to be.
Like the floating river in the form of clouds,
Passing through the endless valley of doubt.

As free as the formless shadow that lingers,
Bound to be enslaved by the presence of light.
Invisibly tethered in a pattern set by society,
Inevitably becoming the epicenter of sorrow.

Something we craft with love and care,
In our imagination, beyond compare,
We guard it with our very soul,
Only to see it take its toll.
The essence of life, in death it lies,
The fear of leaving, the world denies.

40

OCEAN IN THE EYES

Sailing away on the tides of time,
I wonder how you see this world—
As you want it to be,
Or as it wants you to be?

Of all the wisdom I have found,
I feel some of it is left behind.
All my plans, frozen with warmth,
Remain unborn, with no worry to die.

Being washed ashore to reality,
I realize that you are no longer around.
But then I decide to peep into my mind,
Only to find the ocean in the eyes of you.

41

WHISPER OF A DIM LIGHT

A shade of light through the curtain so dim
Reminds me that it's still bright outside.
Blinking my eyes in a motion so slow,
Suspended dust tries to escape the glow.

I hear the birds flapping their wings in joy,
Filling the empty space above my head.
A heart full of freedom caged within their eyes—
Come, little birds, sing me a lullaby.

If I slip into the valley of dreams,
I wish to be asleep forever, just to hear that voice.
The heart is for love, and the mind is to fool,
Like weaving dreams out of cotton and wool.

Volatile feelings are bound to rise;
I will wait, as truth cuts through the lies.

4 2

PARALLEL EXISTENCE

From the lowest mountain peak,

Across the clouds, I seek

A sweetest truth to be,

In everything that I can see.

Even when I'm in joy or feeling low,

Living away from the ones I know.

Strange faces look familiar;

Grief and joy seem so similar.

For how long must the wheel roll?

An endless road my destiny holds.

While shifting my thoughts from left to right,

I tend to dream in black and white.

I, too, exist like you in the speck of time,

Moving ahead with the wind so fine.

As I turn to search for your trace,

A message arrives, and I see your face.

4 3

THE STAR BEHIND MY SKY

Not for the one who means so much,
But for the one who's hard to catch.
It would be easy if I were a tree,
Only to win your trust in me.

I have been restless all this while;
Now I am fine, for it was your smile.
What we want isn't always what we need;
Born as human is the will to give.

Yesterday was good, and we had fun;
Today's been beautiful under the sun.
Tomorrow lies behind the veil of hope;
To view you as a star without a scope.

44
HIDDEN HEIGHTS

Concealed to be seen only with closed eyes,
A figure visible only in the absence of light.
Her breath absorbed by the pillow, well preserved,
Soothing noise from her outlook, yet she's reserved.

To describe her in words is like chasing the horizon,
Bound to believe in something I've never done.
Sweet complications that arise are worth resolving,
Like the hope of life while the planet was evolving.

Eruption of thoughts that keeps me awake—
In this world full of crisis, what's there to take?
To live is to perish for life to flourish.
Taking my time to outlive my troubles and worries.

4 5

THE DREAMSCAPE

In the depth of my sleep,
The most active I am to keep,
I see the most when I close my eyes,
Different things becoming alike.

Watching the birds
Flying freely in the sky,
Brings clouds to my mind,
And rain through my eyes.

I jump and run,
But I can never move.
It's etched in my mind,
But I can't prove.

Nothing is real when I'm around,
Yet the real world's what I've found.
I find myself in a locked-up space,
But I slip through the wall with no trace.

I'm lost, confused, can't comprehend,

I see colors that have no end.

I met you there,

It's a memory I hold dear.

But when I met you here,

You weren't truly there!

46

THE SPHERICAL CUBE

Moved by the sound, life turns around.
Just for a moment, maybe, and all out of bounds.
Being lost leaves a scope for being found;
The path shouldn't be straight in a world so round.

The rhythm of life echoes through my soul,
A dance of shadows that takes its toll.
As I navigate this labyrinth of dreams,
I seek the meaning hidden in the seams.

Yet, even in the uncertainty, beauty persists,
In fleeting moments, in quiet mists.
For within this sphere lies a story untold,
A treasure of resilience waiting to unfold.

So let the sound guide us, let the echoes play,
In the spherical cube, we will find our way.
Though the path may twist, and the journey confound,
Let us embrace the mystery in a world so round.

47

DISAPPEARING CLOUDS

If thoughts were to fall like raindrops sometimes,
most of them would still flow into the drain.
But then, the world would be a thoughtful place,
filled with the elements of art.

But imagine a world where these thoughts could remain,
Like raindrops clinging to the leaves of a tree,
Where every fleeting moment, every passing reflection,
Stays with us, shapes us, and sets us free.

How much richer the world would be,
If each thought lingered, like the scent of rain,
A canvas of dreams, and a tapestry of mind,
Unveiling beauty that only time could explain.

But thoughts, like clouds, often disappear,
Caught by the wind, lost in the air.
Yet in the traces they leave behind,
Clearing the void and the loss we find.

For the world is a canvas, and thoughts are the brush,
We paint our days, we color our dreams.
Though most thoughts may fade with the rush,
Some will live on, like the flow of streams.

And in the end, the world is a thoughtful place,
Not because we captured every fleeting thought,
But because in the spaces between them,
We find the beauty that can't be bought.

So let the clouds disappear, let the rain fall,
For in their wake, we are left with it all:
The fragments, the echoes, the art of our mind,
A reminder that in loss, we often find.

48

CONTINUUM

Caught in the cycle of dusk and dawn,
I wonder where the passing time has gone.
Holding my breath won't make time slow,
But it traps me in moments that won't let go.

As fast as I am tonight,
Tomorrow still finds me in its light.
No distance is farther than my thoughts' flight,
As they stay in my mind's sight.

Moments last if they may,
Like atoms that drift, but never stray.
To be here is to feel gravity's pull,
While racing through thoughts, both sharp and full.

The things we've lost are left behind,
Like energy, never destroyed, only confined.
But the memories of them stay in our mind,
Carried through time, like waves in the bind.

49

ABSOLVE

Being trapped is different from being housed.
A blindfold that blocks the view yet keeps us aroused.
Deep within the dying hopes, it's the soul that lives.
The world around us is painted with the colors of our beliefs.

For liberation blooms in the cracks of the cage,
Gather some courage to turn the page.
To confront the fears that have held us so tight,
Let's embrace the journey from darkness to light.

As we breathe in the essence of our own reality,
Finding strength in the struggle, clarity in duality.
With each step we take, we reclaim our voice,
In the symphony of existence, let us make our choice.

50

DON'T LEAVE THE GROUND

The particles of dust in the form of you,
deflecting the truth. Silence holds this moment
like it's going to fall, under the influence of your existence.
It takes more than a lifetime to read the stories
we leave out of ourselves.

The body changes, and the mind wanders
to broaden the boundaries of thoughts and beliefs.
Lost are not those who know they are lost;
lost are those who have found themselves
residing right beside their soul.

People we meet are ones we usually come across,
and the ones we know can take ourselves from us.

51

PLUNGE INTO THE OCEAN

Never felt so free, descending before,
Soaring without wings, shifting evermore.
Never knew happiness in shades of blue,
Diving deep into the ocean, I'm renewed.

A shift in perception, a change so clear,
Aware of the depths, a connection near.
Embracing the rhythm, a natural flow,
I bond with the earth, as the waters grow.

From the womb, we first draw breath,
Above the surface, a moment we forget.
Diving now, I feel what must have been,
The world before me, vast and serene.

An escape from gravity's heavy hold,
A break from the routine, the stories untold.
The ocean's song, so deep and true,
Filling my soul with a sense of the new.

52

THE VERDANT WISH

The earth turns green from blue,
Leaves spread wide, no glue in view.
A place where nothing fades or dies,
The earth glows green beneath the skies.

Every tree has veins, like ours,
We cut them down, their life devours.
They rise tall and strong, then softly fall,
Because they don't bleed, we judge them all.

The herb of wisdom burns away,
As humanity's plans lead us astray.
The air is clouded with sacred smoke,
A journey where the roads revoke.

5 3

ELEGANT SENTIENCE

The benignant creation of Mother Nature,

Bestowed upon the Earth's curvature.

Capable of performing varied roles in a lifetime,

You are here to turn this world into a shrine.

You are self-reliant; you are the divine.

Among the many things that set you apart,

The whole galaxy can fit inside your altruistic heart.

It's superfluous for you to compete with others;

It's not worth pursuing, and I plead you to understand.

You've always been deprived of your true caliber;

The pages of history are drowned in such literature.

Not for any good reason that was ever true,

But to feed the ego of some insecure creature.

If this world were ruled by you all,

You would never take it under your control.

For you are the creators by nature;

No one can preserve the value of life any better.

Safer than home is the womb of the earth.
You are the feather that shouldn't be tethered.
Although this world exists amidst dreams and reality,
The presence of humans in it is the source of vitality.

My mournful whispers for those who shape your form,
To linger in the depths of oblivion, untouched by truth.
It's about time now to do the best you should,
To nurture this blue orb with womanhood.

54
WHEN STRENGTH BLOSSOMS IN THE HEART

Shattered hopes can still rebuild,
Liberated souls, no longer chilled.
Turning toward truth, no longer far,
Life becomes a journey, not a war.

Wisdom gained through every stride,
Youth embracing life, no longer terrified.
Romance's warmth now fills the air,
Hope shines bright, beyond despair.

We are dreamers, free from chains,
Bound by love, not by fear or pain.
Unity's power lifts us high,
Together, we reach for the sky.

We've learned from paths we've walked before,
In a world of peace, we seek no more.
Being true to oneself is never a crime—
Embrace life, it's a gift for all time.

5 5

EMBRACING HARMONY

Every joy bloom, untouched by pain,
tears fall gently, a cleansing rain.
Nature's promise whispers, soft, yet clear,
with rivers healing what we hold dear.

Hope's light pours, soothing the soul,
a wellspring of love making us whole.
Together we rise, a bond diverse,
our harmony blessed by the endless universe.

For in each of us, a fire burns bright,
and together, we conquer the darkest night.
With courage, hope, and love as our guide,
we rise, unstoppable, side by side.

56

MIND HEARTED

There is nothing special about you
as long as you are special to yourself.
Magic is a myth if you think
your existence is your choice.
Your existence just happens to be
as random as the things around you—look around.
What makes you worthy is what you are capable
of achieving by yourself, regardless of whether
it is big or small.

5 7

TRIBUTE TO HER ESSENCE

Born from the womb, yet chained by the earth,
Not by beasts, but by men who mock her worth.
Despised and mistreated from cradle to grave,
A flower of courage denied the chance to brave.

She nurtures the world with love untold,
Yet is often cast aside, her story left cold.
Though she holds treasures, more precious than gold,
Her life is a winter, harsh and uncontrolled.

A tyrant may tighten the noose with disdain,
But he earns not her submission, only her pain.
Creator and destroyer, she shapes destiny's flow,
The roots of humanity in her, they grow.

She endures all trials, her grace a light,
Her love sustains us through the darkest night.
Troubled by storms that stir her soul,
Yet she remains the heartbeat of life, whole.

A mother, nature's sacred boon,
Breathing life into the darkest gloom.
A man may explore the stars above,
But it's her strength that anchors love.

5 8

FOOTPRINTS IN THE VOID

I marvel at the wonders of nature,
Holding every life in its grand architecture.
Though I wandered far from my destination,
Each step taught me the art of transformation.

Even when paths seem lost and long,
Hope reminds me to stay strong.
My heart beats on with renewed devotion,
And my soul stirs with deep emotion.

I reached for your hand in trust, not despair,
And found strength in the footprints you left there.
Darkness is lovely where stars shine bright,
Guiding my dreams to take hopeful flight.

5 9

VIOLENT SERENITY

Orange light breaks through dark clouds,
while my thoughts speak louder than my words.
I want to be where you are,
but desires don't always get what they want.

Raindrops fall like a mocking smile,
A storm rages outside, but the chaos is inside.
I lost myself trying to get your attention,
and an old hurt returns, disguised as something new.

The sky is quiet, trees at rest,
following the wind on its journey.
I can't remember how we met,
but I remember how to forget.

Fear fades with the falling rain,
right and wrong no longer remain.
In silence, a gesture, small yet true,
I create peace as the storm breaks through.

6 0

AT SOME POINT IN TIME

With fire and speed, a force arrived,
a protector for the world, keeping it alive.
He fought with power to save the earth,
shielding it from darkness, showing its worth.

The stars gathered close to see his might,
clouds cheered, bringing rain and light.
The sun was young, floating in space,
while the moon counted time, lost in its place.

The earth was once a garden of peace,
oceans deep and blue, a calm release.
Forests thrived, untouched by flame,
and even deserts were green, nature's claim.

61

SUSPENDED THOUGHTS

Into the vast, endless blue,
my thoughts take flight, so pure, so true.
Alone, I am free from hate's hold,
as feelings light up fate's story untold.

My soul rises beyond all fight,
finding peace, soaring beyond the night.
Sleep lifts me high into the sky,
the higher I go, the more doubts arise.

A peaceful place, devoid of love,
hanging by the floor, yet nothing above.
All things fall, like trees in the woods,
struggling for life, misunderstood.

Hope's blade strikes with burning fire,
as man's greed consumed by his desire.

62

FRAGMENTS OF LIFE

A piece of land, a drop of water,
And a breeze of air is what matters.
The muted universe of healing sound,
Dynamic objects flying around.

Particles suspended, like peace amidst violence,
A mighty hollow space evolving in silence.
How bright it could have been,
Those colors of flames and planets in between.

To uphold rituals and beliefs held tight,
Yet not a soul could stop the trees from their plight.
Mortal lives dedicated to preservation,
Bound by forces beyond our contemplation.

Beyond the horizon, where sight cannot reach,
Every ray of light carries a lesson to teach.
We dwell in a fragile spark of life,
Claiming to save yet causing pain to survive.

63

THE WEIGHT OF NUMBNESS

When a heart turns into stone,
The warmth of love, now overthrown.
Feelings fail to fill the gaps,
Where once they lived, now silence snaps.
The pulse of life begins to fade,
A distant hum, an echo made.

When the heart turns into a stone,
Feelings falter, leaving gaps unknown.
The floor becomes the looming sky,
Your pulse is a rhythm that won't comply.

No matter how hard you try,
You drown in disbelief, asking why.
The weight of life, too much to bear,
Yet you cannot seem to disappear.
It's like your soul has learned to hide,
While your body drifts with every tide.

No matter how hard you strive,

You sink deeper, barely alive.

Life slips through, a fading plea,

Yet you can't die—you're too busy to be free.

QUANTUM OF TRUTH

The speed of light is constant, but the time we live in stretches and changes in ways we can't fully understand. If I could turn into a beam of light, racing to reach you every day, I would give up everything without a second thought. My journey is restless, always trying to close the distance between us, driven by a deep curiosity to know you better. In this space, I've learned to turn your thoughts into energy—something that can never be created or destroyed, only passed on in an endless cycle of hope that has no limits or time. I know that at some point, life will take us away from each other, but in my mind, you are the galaxy, and I am a wanderer in the vastness of space, floating without direction, without end. Yet, I still feel a quiet happiness, knowing that one day, across the ocean, beyond the sky, and defying gravity's pull, I will find myself in your arms, in a true moment of time and space.

CONCLUSION

The Infinite Dance of Being

As we close the pages of *Bottomless Surface*, we are reminded that the journey through thought, emotion, and existence is never linear. Each poem in this collection, though distinct in its essence, weaves a common thread—a meditation on the complexities and contradictions that define our experience. These verses invite us to look beyond the surface, to explore the depth of our own consciousness, and to embrace the uncertainties that shape us.

This is not the end, but the ongoing journey.

GLOSSARY OF TERMS

1. **Acceptance – Present Tense**
    - **Resistance**: Opposition or a refusal to accept something.
    - **Ebb and flow**: A recurring pattern of movement, like the tides of the sea.
    - **Palette**: A range of colors, used metaphorically here to refer to life's variety of experiences.
2. **Innocent Ignorance**
    - **Beguiling**: Charming or enchanting, often in a deceptive way.
    - **Haunt**: To linger in the memory or mind in an unsettling way.
    - **Terror**: An intense fear, often sudden and overwhelming.
3. **At the Edge of Thought**
    - **Gaze**: A long look or stare, often indicating deep thought.
    - **Music we hear**: Metaphor for the harmony or rhythm in life's moments or experiences.
    - **Fragile**: Easily broken or damaged, often used metaphorically for emotional states or relationships.

4. **Presence of Your Absence**

    - **Tame**: To control or subdue, here referring to the calm after night.
    - **Divine**: Of, from, or like a god; used to refer to something transcendent or spiritual.
    - **Drown**: Overwhelm with emotion or sensation.

5. **Alone in the Sea of Faces**

    - **Guise**: An external appearance, typically used to deceive or mislead.
    - **Imitate**: To copy or follow someone's behavior or actions.
    - **Fate**: The development of events outside a person's control.

6. **The Art of Discussion**

    - **Dialogue**: A conversation or exchange of ideas.
    - **Discord**: Lack of agreement or harmony.
    - **Harmony**: A state of agreement or peaceful coexistence.

7. **Dreams Within Reach**

    - **Afflictions**: Physical or mental conditions that cause pain or suffering.
    - **Fractured**: Broken or damaged, often used metaphorically for the heart or emotions.

8. **793001**
   - **Plateaus**: Flat elevated land areas.
   - **Dew**: Moisture condensed from the air, typically during cool nights.
   - **Guiding star**: A metaphor for a source of direction or hope.
9. **Reverse Horizons**
   - **Frozen sea**: A metaphor for stasis or lack of movement.
   - **Tethered**: Tied or bound, often used figuratively for emotional attachments.
   - **Flicker of hope**: A small sign of optimism or potential.
10. **Contrails in My Sky**
    - **Turbulence**: Unsteady air movement, often causing discomfort.
    - **Sur reality**: A sense of being disconnected from reality, dreamlike.
    - **Altitude**: The height above the Earth's surface.
11. **Breaking of Noise into the Silence**
    - **Molten rocks**: Hot, liquid rock from volcanoes, symbolizing the force of change.
    - **Shroud**: A cover or cloak, often referring to darkness or concealment.

- **Funeral pyre:** A structure used for burning the body in funeral rites, symbolizing the end of something.
- **Bemused:** Confused or lost in thought.

12. **Blessed Enough**
    - **Essence:** The intrinsic nature or indispensable quality of something or someone.
    - **Intertwine:** To twist together, symbolizing a deep connection.
    - **Tension:** The mental or emotional strain that results from conflict or opposing forces.
13. **Veils of Shadows**
    - **Mist:** A fine spray or fog, symbolizing uncertainty or the unknown.
    - **Haunting:** A lingering presence or memory that is difficult to shake off.
    - **Dire:** Urgent, extreme, or critical, often referring to difficult situations.
14. **In Front of the Back**
    - **Crumpled:** To be crushed or bent out of shape.
    - **Shattered:** Broken into pieces, symbolizing emotional or physical ruin.
    - **Tide:** The periodic rise and fall of the sea, symbolizing the flow of emotions or life.

15. **Whispers of the Unconscious**

    - **Torrential**: Used to describe something like a violent downpour, often symbolizing overwhelming emotions.
    - **Hollow**: Empty or meaningless, often referring to emotional emptiness.
    - **Ignites**: To start something, especially a strong reaction or emotion.

16. **Echoes of Existence**

    - **Ageless**: Timeless, not subject to aging.
    - **Frozen water**: Ice, symbolizing emotional numbness or stagnation.
    - **Illusions**: False perceptions or beliefs, often hiding the truth.

17. **The Silent Collapse**

    - **Snare**: A trap or a situation from which it's difficult to escape.
    - **Despair**: The complete loss or absence of hope.
    - **Steel and pearls**: A metaphor for materialism replacing nature and life's simpler beauties.

18. **Ruled by Time**

    - **Gusts of wind**: Sudden bursts of wind, symbolizing changes or disruptions in life.
    - **Bottomless pit**: A metaphor for deep emotional or existential emptiness.

- **Battle**: Referring to life as a constant struggle or challenge.

19. **Nocturnal Embrace**
    - **Diamonds**: Often symbolizes beauty and value, used here to describe the stars.
    - **Revolution**: Refers to a single cycle of the day, symbolizing the passage of time.
    - **Doomsday**: The final day of reckoning, often symbolizing ultimate consequences.

20. **The Illusion of Truth**
    - **Fragments**: Small, broken parts of a whole, symbolizing incomplete knowledge or memory.
    - **Solitude**: The state of being alone, often used here to describe emotional isolation.
    - **Scrawled**: Written hastily or carelessly.

21. **The Essence Unspoken**
    - **Timeless beauty**: A beauty that endures forever, unaffected by time.
    - **Eternal flame**: A symbol of lasting life or love, often used to represent something that never dies.
    - **Value is worth more than gold**: A metaphor for something priceless, beyond material wealth.
    - **Measured by land**: A reference to how people often measure worth by wealth or possessions, which contrasts with the speaker's belief in intrinsic value.

22. **The Modern World**

- **Sacrificial nights**: Nights spent in suffering or loss, often symbolizing the cost of survival.
- **Piercing pain**: Intense emotional or physical pain.
- **Culprits**: Those responsible for wrongdoing, often referring to individuals or systems that perpetuate harm.
- **Diversion**: The act of distracting or misleading, often used to describe the manipulation of truth.
- **Sold**: The idea that everything, including life and values, has been commodified in the modern world.

23. **Undefined**

- **Flames of agony**: Intense emotional or physical suffering.
- **Joy and sorrow lie beside you**: The duality of emotions, always present together.
- **Concealed in the mind**: Referring to emotions or truths that are hidden deep within oneself.
- **Bliss in ignorance**: Finding peace or happiness in not knowing or avoiding difficult truths.

24. **Reflections at Dusk**

- **Fracture in stillness**: An image of disruption in an otherwise peaceful scene, possibly indicating inner conflict.

- **Shadows rise**: The idea that doubts and fears grow as the day transitions into night.
- **Truth murmurs, untold**: The idea that truth exists but is not always expressed openly.

25. **The Grave of Aspirations**

- **Stewards of a world**: Refers to people who are responsible for the care of the Earth, but have failed in this duty.
- **Wounds on the earth**: A metaphor for environmental damage caused by human actions.
- **Restless mind**: A mind filled with turmoil or longing.
- **Ship of dreams**: A symbol for hope or aspiration, often referring to something that has been lost or is in danger.

26. **April Flower: PCD**

- **Numbness**: Emotional or physical numbness, often used to describe the feeling of detachment or emptiness.
- **Shallow breath**: A metaphor for a sense of suffocation or emotional weight.
- **Under the spell**: Being deeply enamored or captivated by someone.

27. **Boundless Affection**

- **Ocean waves**: A metaphor for the expansive and boundless nature of love and care.

- **Branch of endless tree**: A symbol of growth and connection, referring to an ever-lasting relationship.
- **Particles of dust**: A humble metaphor for the speaker's desire to be close to the person they love, to be as small yet meaningful as dust in their presence.

28. **The Journey Towards Light**
    - **Hands of time**: A reference to the passage of time and its inevitable influence on life.
    - **Old ways**: The past habits, beliefs, or actions that must be shed to grow.
    - **Kindness**: An essential quality for creating a better future, as mentioned in the last line.

29. **Lessons of Solitude**
    - **Mountain peak**: A metaphor for the highest point of achievement or introspection, from where one gains perspective.
    - **Wheel roll**: Refers to the cyclical nature of life and fate, a journey that continues regardless of individual desires.
    - **Exiled**: A feeling of emotional or mental isolation, being distant from the world or self.

30. **Specters of the Soul**
    - **Fading away**: A metaphor for losing one's sense of self or purpose.

- **Invisible ropes**: Symbolizes feelings of being trapped or restricted by invisible forces, often emotional or psychological.
- **Cold winds blow**: A metaphor for isolation, emotional numbness, or the harshness of life's journey.
- **Grave inside my heart**: The emotional weight of loss or unhealed grief.

31. **Beyond Redemption**

- **Silver spoon**: A symbol of privilege or being born into wealth, often contrasted with hardship or struggle.
- **No hands but a silver spoon**: Represents someone who has everything handed to them, yet lacks the ability to truly shape their destiny or experience life's challenges.
- **Silver spoon:** Refers to someone born into wealth, but lacking agency or responsibility.
- **Killing for judgment**: A reference to moral and ethical dilemmas, emphasizing the illegitimacy of violence in the name of justice.

32. **Voices of the Void**

- **Mist from the rain**: A metaphor for the blending of different elements in nature, creating something beautiful (a rainbow) out of something seemingly ordinary.

- **Captivated by words so hollow**: Feeling deceived or empty from superficial language or ideas that fail to bring true meaning or fulfillment.
- **Ambush**: A sense of impending danger or conflict, possibly reflecting societal or personal turmoil.
- **Nature be led**: A call to return to nature, abandoning the destructive tendencies of human conflict.

33. **Circles of Thoughts**

- **Cycle spun in endless bends**: Refers to repetitive, circular thinking that seems never-ending, causing mental distress or confusion.
- **Lightning burns my fingertips**: A vivid metaphor for intense experiences or realizations that are both electrifying and painful.
- **Desert, but my feet are wet**: Represents confusion or contradictory emotions, like feeling out of place or in a state of discomfort.
- **All things descend**: A meditation on the inevitability of decline or failure, even for what we try to preserve.

34. **Beauty Beyond Understanding**

- **Charm in ugliness**: Suggests finding beauty in imperfection or unexpected places.
- **Whisper lost in a world so round**: A symbol of how insignificant or unnoticed one can feel in the vastness of the world.

- **Too late to see the truth behind the lies**: Reflects the regret of not realizing truth until after it is too late.

35. **Light and Shadows**
    - **Echoing empty words**: The idea of words spoken without meaning, carrying no substance.
    - **Longing for escape**: The desire to withdraw from the complexities of life and find solace in isolation.
    - **Shadows and light**: The eternal duality, suggesting that both light and darkness play an integral role in our lives.
36. **The Silence of Awareness**
    - **Unawareness**: Refers to the state of ignorance or lack of understanding about one's surroundings or self.
    - **Sheltering behind the veil of ignorance**: Hiding from truth or knowledge to avoid facing uncomfortable realities.
    - **Thoughts flow in reverse**: A metaphor for rethinking or reconsidering one's beliefs or understanding in a non-linear way.
37. **Inward Journey**
    - **Whispers of doubt**: The internal voice of uncertainty that tries to destabilize one's confidence or self-belief.

- **Layers to peel back**: Refers to the layers of the ego or mind that obscure the true self, needing to be shed for self-realization.
- **Spirit bold**: Emphasizes strength, courage, and determination to explore the depths of the soul and find inner peace.

38. **Unfelt Yet Seen**

- **Glimmering shine of the moon**: Represents fleeting moments of beauty or enlightenment that are often difficult to grasp or retain.
- **Time as a gift**: A reflection on the fragility of life, suggesting that time is precious, yet we often take it for granted.
- **Burning desires for you to choke upon**: Metaphor for overwhelming longing or unattainable desires that can suffocate or consume the individual.

39. **Paths of Perception**

- **Floating river in the form of clouds**: A metaphor for the ambiguity and fluidity of self-perception, where one's identity is constantly shifting.
- **Invisibly tethered**: The feeling of being bound to societal expectations or patterns that are not immediately visible.
- **Epicenter of sorrow**: Suggests that our constructed identities, while deeply personal, may ultimately bring us pain and sorrow when they are challenged or broken down.

40. **Ocean in the Eyes**

    - **Tides of time**: A metaphor for the ebb and flow of life and emotions, suggesting the unstoppable movement of time.
    - **Ocean in the eyes of you**: The speaker's realization that the other person's emotions or depth of character are reflected in their eyes—possibly symbolizing a sense of loss or longing.

41. **Whisper of a Dim Light**

    - **Volatile feelings**: Refers to emotions that are unpredictable, unstable, or intense, which can rise and fall quickly.
    - **Truth cuts through the lies**: Implies that, in time, the truth will emerge, dispelling any falsehoods or deceptions.

42. **Parallel Existence**

    - **The wheel rolls**: Symbolizes the cycle of life, time, and fate that seems to go on endlessly.
    - **Destiny holds an endless road**: Suggests the sense of an inevitable journey or life path that cannot be escaped.
    - **Dream in black and white**: Represents seeing life in extremes, possibly symbolizing clarity or a rigid perspective.

43. **The Star Behind My Sky**

- **Hard to catch**: Refers to something or someone elusive or difficult to attain, whether emotionally or in terms of relationships.
- **Born as human is the will to give**: Reflects the inherent nature of humanity to be selfless and to give, even when it conflicts with personal desires.
- **Tomorrow lies behind the veil of hope**: Suggests the uncertainty and mystery surrounding the future, hidden beneath layers of optimism.

44. **Hidden Heights**

- **Chasing the horizon**: A metaphor for seeking something unattainable or endlessly elusive.
- **Hope of life while the planet was evolving**: Symbolizes the ongoing potential for growth and transformation amidst life's challenges.
- **Eruption of thoughts**: Refers to overwhelming and disruptive ideas or emotions.

45. **The Dreamscape**

- **Locked-up space**: Represents feelings of confinement or limitations, either physically or mentally.
- **Slipping through the wall**: Metaphor for escaping boundaries or overcoming restrictions, possibly indicating the surreal nature of dreams.

- **Colors that have no end**: Imagery that conveys a sense of infinity or timelessness, typical of the boundless possibilities of dreams.

46. **The Spherical Cube**

- **Life turns around**: Refers to the cyclical and ever-changing nature of existence.
- **Spherical cube**: A paradoxical image, symbolizing a space where multiple possibilities or dimensions coexist.
- **Dance of shadows**: Refers to life's complex interplay of light and darkness, symbolizing contrasts between good and bad, clarity and confusion.
- **Labyrinth of dreams**: Suggests complexity and confusion, where meaning and direction are unclear, much like navigating through dreams.

47. **Disappearing Clouds**

- **Raindrops clinging to the leaves**: A metaphor for how fleeting thoughts or moments can have lasting impacts if allowed to remain.
- **Fragments, echoes, and art of the mind**: Emphasizes how transient thoughts leave behind traces of meaning, like pieces of art that emerge from the mind's reflection.
- **Canvas of dreams**: Symbolizes the mind as a space where dreams, thoughts, and creativity are painted, representing a world shaped by imagination.

48. **Continuum**

- **Dusk and dawn**: Represents the passage of time, where one cycle ends and another begins.
- **Atoms that drift**: Implies the continuous flow of life, memories, and experiences, all interconnected.
- **Memories stay like waves**: A metaphor for how memories persist, like waves of the ocean that continually wash ashore.

49. **Absolve**

- **Liberation blooms in the cracks of the cage**: Suggests that freedom and personal growth often arise from difficult or confining situations.
- **Duality**: Refers to the coexistence of opposites, such as light and darkness, good and bad, or hope and despair.
- **Symphony of existence**: A metaphor for life itself, where each individual plays a role in the greater harmony of existence.

50. **Don't Leave the Ground**

- **Particles of dust in the form of you**: Refers to the fleeting, impermanent nature of life, particularly in the context of relationships or individual presence.
- **Silence holds this moment**: Implies that the present moment is delicate, and silence or stillness can preserve it.

- **People we meet take ourselves from us**: Suggests that interactions and relationships can alter or change our perception of self, potentially leading to loss or transformation.

51. **Plunge into the Ocean**

- **Ocean**
  - **Meaning**: A vast body of water that symbolizes depth, emotional exploration, and renewal.
  - **Context**: Represents a space of freedom, cleansing, and connection to nature in *"Plunge into the Ocean"*.
- **Rebirth**
  - **Meaning**: The process of being born again or renewed.
  - **Context**: Implied in *"Plunge into the Ocean"*, where diving into the ocean symbolizes emotional and spiritual renewal.

52. **The Verdant Wish**

- **Green/Leaves/Herb of Wisdom**
  - **Meaning**: Represents life, growth, wisdom, and connection to nature.
  - **Context**: Themes of nature's beauty and the consequences of human actions, particularly in *"The Verdant Wish"*.

- **Injustice**
  - **Meaning**: Lack of fairness or righteousness.
  - **Context**: Seen in *"The Verdant Wish"*, highlighting the mistreatment of nature and the destruction of resources.

53. **Elegant Sentience**

- **Self-Reliance**
  - **Meaning**: The ability to depend on oneself for survival and success.
  - **Context**: In *"Elegant Sentience"*, it refers to human independence and the divine nature of self-reliance.
- **Divine Creation**
  - **Meaning**: The belief in a higher power or force behind the creation of life and the universe.
  - **Context**: Described in *"Elegant Sentience"*, referring to the divine nature within humans and the universe.

54. **When Strength Blossoms the Heart**

- **Heart**
  - **Meaning**: Symbolizes love, emotion, vitality, and strength.
  - **Context**: Explored in *"When Strength Blossoms the Heart"* as a place where healing, hope, and unity can be found.

- **Strength**
    - **Meaning**: The quality of being strong in both body and spirit.
    - **Context**: Symbolizes resilience and personal growth, particularly in *"When Strength Blossoms the Heart"*.
- **Unity**
    - **Meaning**: The state of being united or joined as a whole.
    - **Context**: Referenced in *"When Strength Blossoms the Heart"* as a force that lifts individuals to achieve their highest potential.

55. **Embracing Harmony**

- **Harmony**
    - **Meaning**: A state of peaceful coexistence, balance, and unity.
    - **Context**: Central to *"Embracing Harmony"*, where the strength of love and unity can heal and elevate individuals and communities.
- **Cleansing Rain**
    - **Meaning**: Rain that symbolizes renewal, purification, and emotional release.
    - **Context**: Featured in *"Embracing Harmony"* as a metaphor for emotional healing.

56. **Mind Hearted**

- **Existence**
    - **Meaning**: The state of being alive or present, often questioned in terms of purpose or significance.
    - **Context**: In *"Mind Hearted"*, existence is framed as random, urging a focus on individual capability.
- **Ego**
    - **Meaning**: A person's sense of self-importance or self-worth.
    - **Context**: Challenged in *"Mind Hearted"*, where the poem suggests the ego's limitations in understanding true existence.

57. **Tribute to Her Essence**

- **Womanhood**
    - **Meaning**: The state or qualities of being a woman, often tied to strength, nurturing, and creation.
    - **Context**: Celebrated in *"Tribute to Her Essence"*, where the divine feminine is central to life, strength, and nurturing.
- **Sacredness**
    - **Meaning**: The quality of being revered or regarded as holy.

- **Context**: Explored in *"Tribute to Her Essence"*, where nature and womanhood are viewed as sacred and vital to existence.

- **Sacrifice**
  - **Meaning**: The act of giving up something valued for the sake of something greater.
  - **Context**: Referenced in *"Tribute to Her Essence"*, where the sacrifice of women is acknowledged and mourned.

58. **Footprints in the Void**

- **Footprints**
  - **Meaning**: A symbol of guidance, legacy, or journey.
  - **Context**: Represents influence and enduring impact, as explored in *"Footprints in the Void"*.
- **Tides**
  - **Meaning**: The rising and falling of sea levels, symbolizing change and cycles.
  - **Context**: Referenced in *"Footprints in the Void"* to represent the ebb and flow of life's challenges.
- **Transformation**
  - **Meaning**: A profound change in form, structure, or character.
  - **Context**: Explored in *"Footprints in the Void"*, symbolizing personal evolution and the lessons learned from life's journey.

59. **Violent Serenity**

- **Storms and Rain**
  - **Meaning**: Represents inner turmoil, cleansing, and change.
  - **Context**: Featured in *"Violent Serenity"*, where external storms mirror internal emotional chaos.
- **Peace**
  - **Meaning**: The absence of conflict and the presence of serenity.
  - **Context**: Central to *"Violent Serenity"*, where peace is created amidst emotional conflict and turmoil.

60. **At Some Point in Time**

- **Stars**
  - **Meaning**: Represent destiny, guidance, or a source of light in the dark.
  - **Context**: In *"At Some Point in Time"*, stars symbolize cosmic guidance and the universe's role in the human story.
- **Creation vs. Destruction**
  - **Meaning**: The opposing forces of building and tearing down.
  - **Context**: Touched upon in *"At Some Point in Time"*, where nature's balance is sustained by forces of creation and destruction.

61. **Suspended Thoughts**

- **Fate**
  - **Meaning**: The predetermined course of events or destiny.
  - **Context**: Seen in *"Suspended Thoughts"*, where fate is tied to the randomness of existence.
- **Hope**
  - **Meaning**: A feeling of expectation and optimism for the future.
  - **Context**: A driving force in *"Suspended Thoughts"* and *"Footprints in the Void"*, giving individuals the strength to overcome adversity.
- **Peace**
  - **Meaning**: The absence of conflict and the presence of serenity.
  - **Context**: Explored in *"Suspended Thoughts"*, where peace is found in stillness and solitude.

62. **Fragments of Life**

- **Nature's Healing**
  - **Meaning**: The restorative power of nature to mend emotional and physical wounds.
  - **Context**: A theme in *"Fragments of Life"*, where nature's cycles continue despite human interference.

- **Void**
    - **Meaning**: An empty or unfilled space, often symbolic of emptiness or unfulfilled potential.
    - **Context**: Seen in *"Fragments of Life"*, where the void represents the unexplored and neglected aspects of life.

63. **The Weight of Numbness**

- **Numbness**
    - **Meaning**: A state of emotional or physical numbness, often due to trauma or grief.
    - **Context**: Explored in *"The Weight of Numbness"*, where emotional numbness is compared to the heavy burden of life's challenges.
- **Stone**
    - **Meaning**: Represents hardness, coldness, or emotional detachment.
    - **Context**: Used in *"The Weight of Numbness"*, where the heart turning to stone symbolizes the inability to feel or connect.

Inspirations and Literary Context

- **Romanticism**: The theme of nature, emotions, and individual experience might remind one of Romantic poets like William Wordsworth, who often explored the connection between human feelings and the natural world.

- **Transcendentalism**: The sense of connection to nature, self-exploration, and the focus on the present moment in poems such as *Acceptance – Present Tense* resonates with transcendental writers like Ralph Waldo Emerson and Henry David Thoreau.
- **Modern Free Verse**: The poems' use of free verse (lack of consistent rhyme or meter) suggests influences from modern poets like Walt Whitman or contemporary free verse poets.
- **Existentialism**: Poems like *Reverse Horizons* question the nature of existence and the search for meaning, a common theme in existential philosophy and literature.
- **Existentialist Literature**: The questions surrounding identity, meaning, and isolation found in *Echoes of Existence* and *The Illusion of Truth* suggest an influence from existential philosophy, akin to writers like Jean-Paul Sartre or Franz Kafka.
- **Modern Poetry and Free Verse**: The poems employ free verse, not bound by formal rhyme or meter, in a modern poetic style. This makes them similar to poets like Walt Whitman or contemporary poets who focus on emotional expression and personal experience.
- **Surrealism and Symbolism**: Some of these poems (like *Veils of Shadows* and *Echoes of Existence*) employ surreal or symbolic language, borrowing techniques from the Symbolist movement, where abstract

emotions are depicted through vivid, often mystifying imagery.

- **Existential Struggles**: Several poems, such as *Specters of the Soul* and *Undefined*, reflect an ongoing search for meaning, with questions about life, existence, and identity at their core. The idea of loss and the search for purpose is central.
- **Love and Loss**: Poems like *April Flower: PCD* and *Boundless Affection* convey intense emotional connections, but also the pain of separation or unreciprocated love.
- **The Corruption of Society**: In *The Modern World* and *The Grave of Aspirations*, there is a strong critique of contemporary life, greed, and societal decay, highlighting how materialism and corruption affect both the individual and the collective.
- **Hope and Redemption**: Poems such as *The Journey Towards Light* and *Reflections at Dusk* balance darker themes with hope, suggesting that growth and change are possible despite struggles.
- **Modern Dystopian Critique**: *The Modern World* echoes concerns of contemporary society, highlighting the negative impact of greed, corruption, and moral decay, much like dystopian literature that critiques current societal flaws.
- **Existential Reflection**: Many poems explore themes of identity, perception, and the nature of existence,

such as in *Inward Journey*, *The Silence of Awareness*, and *Paths of Perception*. These poems emphasize the complexities of understanding oneself and the world, often focusing on contradictions and the search for inner truth.

- **Isolation and Escape**: A strong sense of detachment from the world is evident in poems like *Voices of the Void*, *Light and Shadows*, and *Unfelt Yet Seen*, where the speaker longs to escape human society and find solace in solitude or nature.
- **The Fragility of Life**: In poems like *Beyond Redemption* and *Ocean in the Eyes*, life is portrayed as fragile and fleeting. The inevitability of death and the impermanence of life are recurring concerns, driving home the importance of appreciating the present.
- **The Duality of Beauty and Pain**: Several poems, such as *Beauty Beyond Understanding* and *Circles of Thoughts*, grapple with the coexistence of beauty and suffering. These poems suggest that pain and beauty are often intertwined, making both essential to understanding the full spectrum of existence.
- **Transience and the Passage of Time:** Several poems reflect on the fleeting nature of thoughts, memories, and life itself. Poems like Disappearing Clouds and Continuum contemplate the passage of time, the impermanence of moments, and the inevitability of change.

- **Duality and Contrast**: Poems such as Parallel Existence and The Spherical Cube explore the idea of contradictions within life, where joy and grief, light and shadow, coexist, offering a complex and multifaceted view of reality.
- **Search for Meaning and Self-Discovery:** Absolve and The Star Behind My Sky focus on personal growth, confronting fears, and finding clarity. These poems suggest that self-liberation often comes through inner struggles and external challenges.
- **The Mystical Nature of Dreams:** Poems like The Dreamscape and Whisper of a Dim Light delve into the surreal, dream-like quality of existence, exploring the blurring of boundaries between reality and imagination.

References and Literary Elements

- **Themes:**
    - **The Struggle for Self**: Poems such as *Blessed Enough* and *Breaking of Noise into the Silence* reflect the complexity of personal identity, emotional vulnerability, and the pursuit of self-knowledge amidst external pressures.
    - **Nature and its Transformation**: Several poems engage with the symbolic use of nature, such as the "molten rocks" in *Breaking of Noise into the Silence* and the "fireflies' glow" in *The Silent*

Collapse, showing how nature mirrors internal emotional states.

- **Existentialism and Meaning**: Poems like *Echoes of Existence* and *The Illusion of Truth* explore themes of searching for purpose and confronting existential doubts.
- **Time and Change**: The passage of time and its impact on the individual is explored in poems such as *Ruled by Time* and *Nocturnal Embrace*, which address the cyclical nature of life and the inevitable passage of time.

- **Symbolism:**
  - **Light and Darkness**: The recurring imagery of light and darkness represents clarity vs. confusion, truth vs. illusion, and hope vs. despair. In *Nocturnal Embrace*, darkness is used to describe the speaker's way of life, while in *Whispers of the Unconscious*, light is a fleeting hope.
  - **Masks and Illusions**: Several poems, such as *Echoes of Existence*, use the motif of a "mask" to represent how one hides their true self from the world or even themselves. The theme of illusion also surfaces in *The Illusion of Truth.*
  - **Isolation and Connection**: Many poems, like *Whispers of the Unconscious* and *Blessed Enough*, tackle the tension between emotional solitude

and the longing for connection, often exploring how to reconcile these two forces.

- **The Earth and Nature**: Nature is a recurring theme, from the "ocean waves" in *Boundless Affection* to "wounds on the earth" in *The Grave of Aspirations*, symbolizing both beauty and destruction.
- **Time and Change**: The passage of time is explored in poems like *Reflections at Dusk* and *The Journey Towards Light*, with time acting as a force that shapes life and consciousness.
- **Nature and Elements**: The recurring imagery of nature in poems like *Voices of the Void*, *Unfelt Yet Seen*, and *Light and Shadows* symbolizes the speaker's internal state or a broader reflection on human existence. Rain, the moon, and the ocean are frequently used to evoke moods of serenity, longing, or isolation.
- **Mind and Consciousness**: *The Silence of Awareness* and *Circles of Thoughts* delve into the inner workings of the mind, focusing on awareness, self-doubt, and the cyclical nature of thoughts and emotions.
- **Cycles and Continuums**: Poems like *Continuum* and *Parallel Existence* explore the cyclical nature of time, existence, and identity. The wheel, the cycle of dusk and dawn, and the journey of life

are recurring symbols that suggest the repetitive and ongoing nature of life.

- **Walls and Boundaries**: Many poems, such as *The Dreamscape* and *Absolve*, use walls and boundaries as metaphors for limitations, whether imposed externally or self-inflicted. Overcoming these boundaries is often depicted as a necessary part of personal growth.

- **Literary Devices:**
  - **Metaphor**: A dominant feature in these poems, comparing abstract ideas to tangible objects or actions. For example, *Breaking of Noise into the Silence* uses "molten rocks" as a metaphor for the intensity of change.
  - The use of metaphors is central to these poems, such as *Beyond Redemption*'s "a tree with huge branches and no roots" or *Paths of Perception*'s "floating river in the form of clouds," to convey complex concepts like identity and the search for meaning.
  - **Alliteration and Assonance**: The use of repeating consonant or vowel sounds to create rhythm or emphasize certain themes, such as "Shattered boat drifts without sail" from *In Front of the Back.*
  - **Imagery**: Vivid imagery is prevalent in all the poems, such as "Darkness brightens my way" in

Nocturnal Embrace, helping evoke deep emotional responses from the reader.

- **Personification**: Giving human qualities to non-human things, like the "silent collapse" in *The Silent Collapse* where nature itself seems to reflect the collapse of emotional states.
- The use of metaphors is prominent, such as "a stone that dreams of taking flight" in *Specters of the Soul*, symbolizing unfulfilled desires or potential.
- Giving human qualities to abstract concepts, such as "Truth murmurs, untold" in *Reflections at Dusk*, making the concept of truth seem active and elusive.
- Subtle repetition of sounds is used for emphasis, such as in *The Modern World* ("Sacrificial nights of restless sleep").
- Vivid imagery is used throughout, like "ocean waves" in *Boundless Affection* and "sun rays" in *April Flower: PCD*, creating a strong sensory experience for the reader.
- Vivid imagery is used throughout, especially in poems like *Unfelt Yet Seen* ("Shifting shades of glimmering shine") and *Voices of the Void* ("Mist from the rain creates the rainbow"), creating strong visual impressions that reflect the emotional states of the speaker.

- **Irony**: The use of irony is evident in *The Grave of Aspirations*, where a generation is described as "lost in space," pointing to the disconnect between hope and the reality of modern life.
- Poems like *Circles of Thoughts* and *Beauty Beyond Understanding* explore paradoxical ideas, like finding beauty in ugliness or the cyclical nature of thought, where progress seems impossible.
- The use of metaphors is prevalent in almost every poem, such as *Parallel Existence*'s "wheel rolls" and *The Dreamscape*'s "locked-up space," creating powerful images that capture complex feelings and ideas about identity, time, and experience.
- Rich visual imagery, like in *Whisper of a Dim Light* ("shade of light through the curtain so dim") or *Disappearing Clouds* ("raindrops clinging to the leaves"), helps convey emotional depth and internal states.
- The act of giving human characteristics to inanimate things is common, as seen in *The Spherical Cube* ("rhythm of life echoes through my soul") and *Absolve* ("liberation blooms in the cracks of the cage"), which enhances the abstract qualities of the poems.
- **Rhetorical Questions**: Used in poems like *Continuum* ("Where has the passing time gone?"), these questions invite the reader to contemplate

existential dilemmas and the passage of time, adding an introspective tone to the work.

- Themes of self-discovery, confronting the unknown, and the meaning of life in poems like *Absolve* and *Parallel Existence* suggest influences from existential thought, focusing on the importance of personal freedom and individual meaning.
- The dreamlike quality in *The Dreamscape* and *Whisper of a Dim Light* reflects a surrealist approach, where boundaries between reality and imagination blur, exploring subconscious thoughts and emotions.
- The deep connection to nature, freedom, and emotional expression found in poems like *Whisper of a Dim Light* and *The Star Behind My Sky* reflects the influence of Romantic ideals, which emphasize individual emotion and the beauty of the natural world.
- Repeated words and rhythms help emphasize the ongoing struggles or reflections in poems like Circles of Thoughts ("A cycle spun in endless bends") and Inward Journey ("What others make you feel is not true").

www.ingramcontent.com/pod-product-compliance
Lightning Source LLC
LaVergne TN
LVHW042349150826
845671LV00002B/69

9798897242641